TALES OF ANIMALS

Retold Timeless Classics

Perfection Learning®

Retold by Karen Berg Douglas

Editor: Lisa Owens
Editorial Assistant: Berit Thorkelson
Illustrator: Randy Messer

Text © 1999 by Perfection Learning® Corporation.
All rights reserved. No part of this book may be used or
reproduced in any manner whatsoever without written
permission from the publisher.

For information, contact:
Perfection Learning® Corporation
1000 North Second Avenue, P.O. Box 500
Logan, Iowa 51546-1099
Tel: 800-831-4198 • Fax: 712-644-2392

Paperback ISBN 0-7891-2858-6
Cover Craft® ISBN 0-7807-7852-9
Printed in the U.S.A.

5 6 PP 06 05

Contents

Tale 1: Rikki-Tikki-Tavi 5

Tale 2: The Colony of Cats 17

Tale 3: The Country Mouse and the Town Mouse .. 25

Tale 4: The Fox and the Wolf................. 31

Tale 5: The Lion and the Mouse............... 39

Tale 6: How Some Wild Animals Became Tame ... 43

The Play: How Some Wild Animals Became Tame ... 48

          Act One 49

          Act Two 50

          Act Three 52

Rikki-Tikki-Tavi

A Tale from Rudyard Kipling

He did not look like a mongoose. His fur and his tail made him look like a cat. His head looked like a weasel. And his eyes—and the end of his nose—were pink.

Besides that, he had a funny name. He made a strange sound when he raced through the long, green grass. He said, "Rikk-tikk-tikki-tikki-tavi."

One summer morning, there was a big flood in the small village. It washed the little mongoose out of his home. When he woke up, he was in a garden.

As he lay there, a small boy came down the path with his mother. They picked Rikki-tikki up carefully. Then they carried him into the house.

"Don't frighten him," said the boy's father. "Let's see what he will do."

So they put him in a nice warm bed. Rikki-tikki jumped up and ran around the table. Then he looked at the little boy and jumped up on his shoulder.

TALES OF ANIMALS

"Don't be frightened, Teddy," said the father. "That's his way of making friends."

"Ouch! He's tickling my chin," said Teddy.

Rikki-tikki sniffed at the boy's ear. Then he poked at his hair. Next he jumped to the floor and rubbed his nose.

"He is so tame," said the mother. "Do you suppose that's because we have been kind to him?"

"No. All mongooses are like that," said the father. "Teddy must not pick him up by the tail. And we must not put him in a cage. He likes to be free."

"Let's give him something to eat," said Teddy. "Maybe he's hungry."

They gave him some raw meat. Rikki-tikki liked it very much. When he finished, he went outside. He sat in the sun and fluffed up his fur. He felt better.

Rikki-tikki liked this house. He loved to climb into Teddy's bed at bedtime. When Teddy's mother and father came in, Rikki-tikki was sitting on Teddy's pillow.

"I don't like that," said Teddy's mother. "He may bite."

"No he won't," said his father. "Teddy is safer with that mongoose than he would be with a dog."

And they turned out the lights and went to sleep.

The next morning, Rikki-tikki hopped on Teddy's shoulder. The two went downstairs for breakfast. Teddy gave him some banana and a boiled egg. Then Rikki-tikki went out to the garden.

This is a nice hunting ground, thought the mongoose. And he began to sniff around.

Before long, Rikki-tikki heard two sad voices. It was Darzee, the tailor-bird, and his wife. They were sitting in a beautiful nest.

"What is the matter?" asked Rikki-tikki.

"We are very sad," said Darzee. "One of our babies fell out of the nest. And Nag ate him."

"Hmmm," said Rikki-tikki. "That *is* very sad. But I am new here. Who is Nag?"

But Darzee and his wife didn't get to answer.

Rikki-tikki heard a low hiss in the grass. And he saw who Nag was! Nag was a big, black cobra. He looked at the mongoose with mean snake eyes.

"Who is Nag, you ask?" the snake repeated. "Why, *I* am Nag. Look and be afraid."

Rikki-tikki *was* afraid for a minute. But then he remembered what his mother had taught him. Mongooses were supposed to fight and eat snakes.

Nag knew that too. And in his cold heart, Nag was afraid. But he would not say so.

"Well," said Rikki-tikki, fluffing up his tail. "Do you think it is nice for you to eat little birds out of a nest?"

The snake dropped his head a little and put it to one side. "Well, you eat eggs," he said. "Why should I not eat birds?"

"Behind you! Look behind you!" Darzee cried suddenly.

TALES OF ANIMALS

Rikki-tikki jumped high in the air. Just under him whizzed the head of Nagaina, Nag's wicked wife.

Rikki-tikki came down on her back and bit her.

"Bad, bad Darzee!" said Nag.

Rikki-tikki felt his eyes growing red and hot. This means that a mongoose is very angry.

Rikki-tikki sat back on his hind legs like a little kangaroo. He looked all around. But the snakes were gone. Nag and Nagaina had moved back into the tall, green grass.

Rikki-tikki decided not to follow them. He wasn't sure he could take care of two snakes at once. Instead, he followed the path to the house. He would sit and think about the day.

A few minutes later, Teddy came running out of the house. Rikki-tikki wanted to be petted. But something moved in the dust.

"Be careful. I can hurt you," said a tiny voice.

It was Karait, a dusty brown snake. His bite was as dangerous as the cobra's.

Rikki-tikki's eyes grew red again. He danced up to Karait and rocked and swayed like a mongoose does.

Karait struck out with his head. Rikki-tikki jumped sideways and tried to run.

"Look, look!" Teddy shouted. "Our mongoose is killing a snake."

Teddy's mother screamed. His father grabbed a big stick and ran outside. But it was too late. Rikki-tikki had jumped on Karait's back and bitten him. Teddy's father hit the snake with the big stick.

Rikki-Tikki-Tavi

Rikki-tikki got ready to eat the snake up from the tail. (That's what his mother had taught him.) But then he remembered something. If a mongoose wants to be strong and quick, he must keep himself thin.

Rikki-tikki had already had his breakfast. So he put down the snake. Then he left to take a dust bath under some bushes. Teddy's mother followed him. She picked him up and hugged him.

"You have saved our little Teddy," said the mother.

Rikki-tikki did not understand why she was so happy. But he liked her. And he liked the father and Teddy too.

That night, Rikki-tikki walked around the dinner table. He could have stuffed himself many times with good food. But he kept thinking about Nag and Nagaina.

At bedtime, Teddy carried Rikki-tikki upstairs. As soon as the child was asleep, the mongoose went out for his nightly walk. In the dark, he ran into Chuchundra, the muskrat.

"Don't kill me!" cried Chuchundra. "Don't kill me, Rikki-tikki!"

"Do you think a snake killer kills muskrats?" asked Rikki-tikki.

They both laughed.

"No, but those who kill snakes get killed by snakes, Rikki-tikki," Chuchundra said. "And how am I to be sure that Nag won't mistake me for you some dark night?"

"Nag is in the garden. And I know you don't go there," Rikki-tikki said.

"But my cousin, Chua the rat, told me . . ." said Chuchundra. Then he stopped.

"Told you what?" Rikki-tikki said. "What did Chua tell you?"

"Hush! Nag is everywhere, Rikki-tikki. You should talk to Chua," Chuchundra said.

And with that, he sat down and began to cry. After a few minutes, he began to talk.

"I can't tell you anything, Rikki-tikki," Chuchundra said. "But listen. Can you hear anything?"

Rikki-tikki sat very still and listened. The house was still. But he thought he could hear a scratching noise. It sounded like the dry scratch of a snake's scales on bricks.

"That's Nag or Nagaina," he said to himself. "And I'll bet one of them is crawling into the bathroom."

Rikki-tikki ran back into the house and into Teddy's bathroom. There was nothing there. He ran into Teddy's mother's bathroom. There, at the bottom of the wall, a brick had been pulled out. He heard Nag and Nagaina talking to each other outside in the moonlight.

"Go in quietly," whispered Nagaina. "Remember, bite the man who killed Karait first. Then come out and get me. And we will hunt for Rikki-tikki together."

"But are you sure it is wise to kill them?" said Nag.

"Yes," said Nagaina. "When there are no people in the house, we will be king and queen of the garden. You know, as soon as our eggs hatch, our children will need room and quiet. And they may hatch tomorrow."

"I had not thought of that," said Nag. "But if I kill the man, the woman, and the child, the house will be empty. And Rikki-tikki will go."

Rikki-tikki was angry. But he didn't move. He sat and watched Nag's big head come through the hole. Nag's five feet of body followed it.

Rikki-tikki was afraid.

Nag raised his head and looked into the dark bathroom. Rikki-tikki could see his mean eyes.

Rikki-tikki thought, If I kill him here, Nagaina will know. And if I fight him on the open floor, he may win. What should I do?

Nag took a drink from the water jar. Then he spoke to Nagaina. "When the man comes in for his bath in the morning, he will not have a stick. I will wait here until he comes. Nagaina, do you hear me?"

There was no answer. So Rikki-tikki knew that Nagaina had gone away. Nag wrapped himself around the bottom of the water jar. And Rikki-tikki stayed very still.

After an hour, Nag was asleep. Rikki-tikki looked at his big back, wondering where to take hold of him.

If I don't break his back at the first jump, he can still fight, Rikki-tikki thought. I'll jump on the head. But once I am there, I must not let go!

So Rikki-tikki jumped.

Nag woke up instantly. He was strong. And he began to shake the mongoose up and down—and all around in big circles!

But the mongoose held on. Rikki-tikki was dizzy. His head hurt. His body hurt.

Still, the snake kept shaking him.

Suddenly, there was a loud bang! The snake fell to the floor.

"It's the mongoose again, Alice," said the man. "This little guy has saved *our* lives now."

"What happened?" said the mother.

"I woke up when I heard the noise. I went and got my gun. I found the snake in the bathroom. And I shot him."

Rikki-tikki wasn't sure what had happened. He went to Teddy's bedroom. He just wanted to sleep. When morning came, the mongoose was still sore.

"Now I have Nagaina to take care of," Rikki-tikki said. "And what if the eggs hatch? I must go and see Darzee."

Rikki-tikki didn't wait for breakfast. He ran to the big bush in the garden. Darzee was singing happily. Everyone had heard the news of Nag's death.

"Oh, you silly thing of feathers!" said Rikki-tikki, angrily. "Is this the time to sing?"

"Nag is dead! Nag is dead!" Darzee sang. "He will never eat my babies again!"

"All that's true," Rikki-tikki said. "But where's Nagaina? Do you know where she keeps her eggs? Please stop singing for a minute and tell me."

Rikki-Tikki-Tavi

"Nagaina's eggs are in the melon bed," Darzee said. "She's crying for Nag by the rose garden."

Rikki-tikki needed some help. He asked Darzee to go to the rose garden and talk with Nagaina.

"Well, I suppose I can do that much," said Darzee. And away he flew.

Then Rikki-tikki went to find the eggs.

Nagaina lifted her head when she saw Darzee.

"You told Rikki-tikki that I was going to kill him," Nagaina said. "I don't like you. And let me tell you, I will visit the house again."

Then Nagaina began chasing the bird around the garden.

Rikki-tikki heard them going up the path. He raced to the end of the melon patch. He found 25 eggs there.

He knew that as soon as they hatched, they could kill a man or a mongoose. So he began biting off the tops of the eggs as fast as he could. At last, there were only three eggs left.

Suddenly, Rikki-tikki heard Darzee scream.

"Rikki-tikki! Come quickly!" she cried. "I think Nagaina is going to hurt the boy!"

Rikki-tikki smashed two eggs and ran toward the house. He still had the third one in his mouth. He walked in the door. Teddy and his mother and father were sitting at the table.

They were not eating. Their faces were very white. There, near Teddy's leg, was Nagaina.

"Sit still, Teddy," his father warned. "You must not move."

TALES OF ANIMALS

Rikki-tikki walked up to the snake.

"Turn around, Nagaina," he said. "Turn and fight."

The snake did not move.

"Go look at your eggs," said Rikki-tikki.

The big snake turned and saw the egg on the floor.

"Give it to me," she said.

Rikki-tikki put his paws on the egg. His eyes turned red. Nagaina turned around. This was her egg. This was her baby.

Nagaina tried to get the egg. At that moment, Teddy's father grabbed his son and pulled him away.

"Tricked! Tricked! Tricked! Rikk-tikk-tikk!" Rikki-tikki laughed.

Then he began to jump up and down, his head close to the floor. Nagaina had lost her chance to hurt the boy. Now the egg lay between Rikki-tikki's paws.

"Give me the egg, Rikki-tikki," she demanded. "Give me the last of my eggs. Then I will go away and never come back."

Rikki-tikki jumped here and there. The snake tried to catch him. Then she got hold of the egg. Nagaina slid down the path toward the rat hole where she lived.

Rikki-tikki ran after her, catching her by the tail. He hung on. He didn't let go. The birds watched as Nagaina pulled Rikki-tikki into the hole.

Suddenly, everything was quiet. Darzee began to sing.

"It is all over with Rikki-tikki," he said. "Nagaina will kill him for sure."

Rikki-Tikki-Tavi

But just then, the grass moved again.

Rikki-tikki emerged from the hole. He was covered with dirt.

"It is all over," he said. "She will never come out again. Tell the Coppersmith bird, Darzee. He will tell the rest of the garden that Nagaina is dead."

And with that, Rikki-tikki lay down in the grass and went to sleep.

When he awoke a short time later, Rikki-tikki decided to go back to the house. As he went up the path, the birds sang about the death of the two snakes.

When Rikki got to the house, Teddy and his mother and father came out to hug him.

That night, they gave him a big dinner. When he could eat no more, he jumped up on Teddy's shoulder.

Later, Rikki curled up close to Teddy.

"Just think. He saved our lives," said Teddy's mother to her husband.

Rikki-tikki woke up with a jump. He was happy and proud of himself. He had a right to be.

And from that day on, no cobra ever showed its head inside the garden again.

The Colony of Cats

Once upon a time, there was an old house just outside town. It was filled with hundreds of cats.

No one is sure how they got there. Some say they came when all the mice lived in town. That when the cats moved in, the mice moved away. And the cats stayed on and on and on.

The cats were very happy living together. They always had enough to eat. No one knows where they got the money to pay for everything. But they were able to pay a servant.

The servant cooked their meals and kept the house clean. Sadly, no servant ever stayed very long. Most of them got tired of living alone with the cats. Most of them, that is, until Lizina came along.

Lizina was unhappy at home. Her mother made her work very hard. And her sister, Peppina, did nothing.

One day, Lizina decided to leave home. "I think I will go and live with the cats," she said.

"Oh, be off with you. Just go," said her mother. She didn't think Lizina would really run away from home.

TALES OF ANIMALS

But Lizina ran out the door. She didn't stop running until she got to the cats' house.

The cats were happy to see Lizina. Their cook had just left that morning. They were very hungry. So Lizina went to the kitchen to fix their dinner.

"We must find out more about this young girl," said one of the cats.

One by one, they crept into the kitchen to look at her. One sat at Lizina's feet. Another sat on the back of her chair while she peeled potatoes. And another sat on the table beside her.

They mewed and purred. But Lizina did not understand what they were saying.

Lizina worked very hard to be kind to her new family. She kept the house clean. She cooked good meals. And when the cats were sick, she took care of them.

One morning, there was a knock at the door. Lizina got up from the table to answer it. But just as she got there, in walked a big old cat.

"Hello. My name is Father Gatto," he mewed. "I live up in the old barn at the top of the hill. I just came down to see all my children."

Then he turned to the cats who had gathered. "Is this young black-eyed girl taking care of you?" he asked.

"Oh, yes, Father Gatto," they answered. "We have never had such a good servant."

Each time he came to visit, he asked the same question. And the answer was always the same.

The Colony of Cats

Father Gatto was pleased. But after a few weeks, the old cat saw that Lizina had begun to look sad. One day, he found her crying in the kitchen.

"What is the matter, my child?" he asked. "Has someone been unkind to you?"

"Oh, no, Father Gatto," Lizina answered. "All the cats are very good to me. But I am lonely. And I would like to see my mother and sister."

Old Father Gatto smiled. "Then you must go home," he said. "And do not come back here unless you want to. Now before you go, I want to give you something for being so kind to my children."

Father Gatto took a key from the chain around his neck. Then he opened the door to the cellar and told Lizina to follow him.

At the bottom of the stairs, Lizina looked around in surprise. There were two big jars by the wall. One was filled with oil. The other was filled with gold water.

"I want to dip you into one of these jars," Father Gatto said. "Which one shall it be?"

Lizina looked at the two jars. She could not ask the old cat to dip her in gold. So she chose the jar filled with oil.

"No, no. You deserve something better than that," said Father Gatto.

Then he picked her up in his big paws and dropped her into the jar of gold. A few minutes later, he helped her out.

Lizina was gold from head to toe. And her pockets were filled with gold coins.

TALES OF ANIMALS

"Now go home and see your mother and sister," said Father Gatto. "But take care. If you hear the cock crow, turn toward it. And if the donkey brays, you must look the other way."

Lizina hugged the old cat and kissed his white paw. Then she ran out the door and started for home.

The moment Lizina got to her mother's house, the cock crowed. She turned toward it, just as the old cat had told her to do. Suddenly, a beautiful gold star appeared on her forehead.

At the same time, the donkey began to bray. Lizina looked the other way.

Lizina's mother and sister came out to meet her. They were so happy to see her. Lizina put her hand in her pocket. She drew out a handful of gold for each of them.

Lizina and her mother and sister were happy living together again. Lizina gave them everything she had been given. She wanted to please them.

But soon, Peppina wanted more. So one morning, she got up very early. She took Lizina's basket. Then she walked to the cats' house.

The cats had been sad since Lizina left. They hoped that she would come back to them. So they did not try to find another servant.

When they heard that Peppina was Lizina's sister, they all ran to meet her. The cats were happy. And they welcomed her into their home.

But a few days later, they wanted Peppina to leave.

The Colony of Cats

"Why, she is not at all like Lizina," the kittens whispered.

"No, she is mean," mewed the cats.

One day, Peppina shut the kitchen door. She did not want the tomcats to watch her work. One of the kittens crawled through an open window and jumped on the table. Peppina hit him with a wooden spoon.

The cats were very unhappy.

There was dust in every room. Spiderwebs hung from the ceilings. And the beds were never made.

Father Gatto was surprised when he came to visit.

"Peppina kicked Maude with her wooden shoe," said one cat. "Now she has a sore paw."

"Hector has a sore back because Peppina threw a wooden chair at him," said another.

"Do send her away, Father Gatto!" they all cried.

Father Gatto thought for a moment.

"I have an idea," he said at last.

Father Gatto called to Peppina. When she came into the kitchen, he took her down into the cellar. There were the two big jars that he had showed Lizina.

"I want to dip you into one of these jars," he said. "Which one shall it be?"

"In the gold, of course," said Peppina.

Father Gatto's eyes turned red and yellow like fire.

"You do not deserve it!" he shouted.

With that, he threw her into the jar of oil. When Peppina reached the top, he pulled her out. And he rolled her in ashes. Then he opened the door and threw her out.

TALES OF ANIMALS

"Be gone with you!" shouted Father Gatto. "And when you meet a donkey who brays, turn your head toward it."

Peppina ran away. Soon, she heard a donkey bray. She turned her head to look at it. And something fell in front of her eyes.

Peppina put her hand to her forehead. There, just above her eyes, was a big donkey's tail.

Peppina ran all the way home.

It took Peppina two hours and two cakes of soap to get rid of the oil and ashes. But try as she might, she could not get rid of the donkey's tail.

The girls' mother was very angry.

"It is all your fault," she told Lizina. "Go to the well and sit there."

Lizina began to cry.

Now it just so happens that the king's son was walking by. He saw Lizina sitting by the well. He thought she was so beautiful that he came back three times.

The fourth time, the prince asked Lizina to marry him.

"I will," she answered.

The next day, the prince arrived to get Lizina. He found his bride all wrapped up in a white veil. Of course, it was really Peppina. But the prince did not know that. So he helped her into the carriage.

Peppina sat very still. She did not say a word.

A short way down the road, they passed the cats' house. The cats knew what had happened. So when they saw the carriage, they began to sing:

"Mew, mew, mew!
Prince, look quick behind you!
By the well is fair Lizina,
And you have nothing but Peppina!"

When the carriage driver heard the cats, he stopped the horses. He turned to the prince. And he asked, "Do you understand what the cats are saying?"

The cats sang louder.

The prince threw back the veil. There was Peppina. The donkey's tail was still on her head.

"Turn around," the prince told the driver. "I am taking this girl back to her mother."

When they reached the house, the prince jumped out of the carriage.

"Where is my bride?" he demanded.

The old woman began to cry. "I will take you to her," she said.

When they reached Lizina, the prince put his arms around her.

"You will come home with me," he said. "I will take care of you."

A few days later, Lizina and the prince were married. It was a beautiful day. The sun was shining. And there was lots of good food to eat.

And all the cats, even old Father Gatto, were at the wedding.

The Country Mouse and the Town Mouse

A Tale from Aesop

Once upon a time, if you looked very close, you could see it. It was a tiny hole in the stones of a wall. This was where Country Mouse and his wife lived.

They were very happy. Every fall, they went into the fields and picked wheat. Sometimes, they got berries from the bushes. Or acorns from the oak tree. They thought they lived like a king and a queen.

One day while eating breakfast, they began to think about Town Mouse.

TALES OF ANIMALS

"You know, I think we should invite him for a visit," said Country Mouse. "He might like to see how well we live."

"You are right," said the wife. "Let's ask him to come this week."

A few days later, Town Mouse arrived at their door.

"Do come in," said Country Mouse. "We are so happy to see you!"

Country Mouse showed Town Mouse his home. He showed off his children. Then he went to the cupboard. He brought out the berries and acorns and wheat.

His wife brought out some crab apples and sweet, white nuts.

"Eat, eat! As much as you want!" said Country Mouse.

Town Mouse looked down his whiskers. "Is this all you have?" he asked, with a shake of his tail.

"This is very good food!" said Mrs. Country Mouse. "My husband worked hard to get it. Why, I'm sure no mouse in the world has a cupboard as full as mine!"

"Dear lady," said Town Mouse. "This may be all right for the country. But in town, we eat even better!"

Mrs. Country Mouse was angry. She took all the food from the table. "Well, then. We will eat this another day," she said.

But her husband wanted to know more.

"Tell me, how do you live?" asked Country Mouse.

The Country Mouse and the Town Mouse

"You must visit me and find out," said Town Mouse.

So a few days later, Country Mouse brushed his fur and washed his feet and tail. And he started off for the city. Town Mouse met him in the field.

"Now, be careful, my dear cousin," said Town Mouse. "When you're in the city, you can't let anyone see you. And you have to be very quiet."

So the two mice crept into the big house where Town Mouse lived.

It was a beautiful house with warm rugs on the floor. There was nice furniture to climb. In the dining room was one tiny hole in the wall. That was where Town Mouse lived.

"I think they are getting ready to serve a big dinner," said Town Mouse. "Before I show you my house, let's get something to eat."

With that, the two mice climbed up the white lace tablecloth onto the big table. Oh, such fine food they saw!

There was ham. And potatoes. There were peas and carrots and fresh wheat rolls. Why, there was even a big round of cheese!

"What do you think of this?" said Town Mouse.

"Oh, my," Country Mouse replied. "I don't know where to begin!"

"Try that ham," said Town Mouse.

TALES OF ANIMALS

Country Mouse ran to the other side of the table. But just as he put his tiny foot on the plate, the door to the kitchen opened! In came many happy, hungry people!

With a squeak, Town Mouse ran down the tablecloth and into the hole. Country Mouse followed him.

"Whew! I haven't run that fast in a long time," said Country Mouse.

"Shhhh. Be very quiet now," said Town Mouse. "If they know we are here, they will kill us."

The two mice peeked out the hole. They watched the happy people eat up most of the good food.

"Don't worry, dear cousin," said Town Mouse. "They will leave some for us."

Finally, the people stopped eating. They went to another room to talk. So the two mice crept out of the hole and ran up the tablecloth onto the table again.

They had just started to take some ham when the door opened!

In came a servant with two big dogs. "Mice! Mice!" he shouted. "We have mice!"

The two dogs began to bark. The mice ran across the table, down the lace tablecloth, and into the hole.

"Whew! We made it," said Town Mouse.

"But I'm still hungry," Country Mouse replied. "Fine food is nice, dear cousin. But if you can't eat it, what use is it? I'm going home."

"Well then, be gone with you," said Town Mouse.

And with a shake of his tail, Country Mouse was gone.

"My family and I will stay where we are," he said happily. As he ran down the road, he added, "We will eat wheat and berries and acorns every day. And no one will get after us!"

No one knows what happened to Town Mouse. But Country Mouse and his family lived happily ever after. And they never went back to the city again.

The Fox and the Wolf

Many years ago, there was a quiet little village at the base of a big mountain. There were two roads in and out of the village. One went east and the other went west.

One summer night, a big wolf came walking down the road.

"I must get a good dinner before I go back to my den," he said to himself. "It has been a week since I had a good meal."

Of course, there were lots of rabbits in the mountains. But the wolf was getting old. He could not run as fast as he once did. Many of the rabbits could run faster.

"I would be so happy if I could catch that fox I saw," said the wolf. "But everyone knows that foxes run as fast as the wind."

While the wolf was thinking about the fox, the fox was coming down the other road.

"I have listened to the chickens cluck all day," the fox said to herself. "That's a nice thing to hear. Especially when you like chickens and eggs as much as I do. I am so hungry. I think I will try to catch some for dinner."

Just then, the fox came to the place where the two roads met.

"I think I will take a little rest under this nice tree," she said. And she lay down to sleep.

A few minutes later, the wolf came by.

"Here is my dinner," he thought, moving a little closer. "But oh, my, she is very thin."

Now a fox has very good ears. She heard the wolf as he moved through the grass. So she called to him.

"Is that you, neighbor?" the fox asked. "I hope you are quite well."

"Quite well, indeed," the wolf answered. "At least as well as one can be when one is very hungry. But what is the matter with you? You are so thin."

The Fox and the Wolf

"I have been sick. Very sick," said the fox. "What you say is true. A worm is fat. Much fatter than I am."

"Indeed," the wolf said. "But you still look good enough to eat."

"Oh, you are always joking," the fox said. "I am sure you are not half as hungry as I am."

"We will see," said the wolf, opening his mouth.

"What are you doing?" cried the fox. She jumped up and stepped back.

"Why, I am going to eat you for supper," the wolf said.

"Well, I suppose you must have your joke," said the fox.

"I don't want to joke," said the wolf. "I am hungry. I want to eat."

"But once you eat me, it will feel like you ate nothing at all," the fox said.

"Now just a minute," the wolf said. "I don't want to talk to you. I want to eat you up."

The fox began to cry. She wiped her eyes with her tail. "Have you not pity for a poor mother?" she said.

"But I am so hungry," the wolf said.

"Well, before you eat me up, let me tell you a story," the fox said.

"Okay. But be quick about it. I will fall down on my face if I have to wait much longer."

And with that, the fox began her tale.

TALES OF ANIMALS

"In this village," she began, "there is a rich man. He makes lots of cheese every summer. He keeps the cheese in a dry old well. Two buckets hang nearby. I have gone there many nights. I let myself down in the bucket. And I bring home enough cheese to feed my children."

The wolf sat still as the fox continued her story.

"Please come with me," said the fox. "Please let me make a good meal of the cheese before I die."

The wolf looked at the fox's thin body. Maybe the cheese will fatten her up, he thought. Then she will make a better dinner for me.

"Lead the way," the wolf said. "But I must warn you. Do not try to get away or play any tricks."

The fox and the wolf crept down the road toward the rich man's house. Suddenly, they stopped and looked at each other. They smelled something cooking. Bacon! It smelled so good, and they both were so hungry.

As they walked on, some dogs barked.

"Do you think it's safe to go on?" asked the wolf.

The fox shook her head. "Not while the dogs are barking," she said. "Someone might come out and see us. Let's wait a little while."

Soon the dogs stopped. And the fox and the wolf jumped up. They ran to the wall around the rich man's house.

I am smaller than the wolf, thought the fox. If I run, I can get a good start. And I can jump over the wall first.

The Fox and the Wolf

But the wolf could jump fast too. He jumped right beside her.

"What were you going to do, my friend?" asked the wolf.

"Oh, nothing," she said. "I just thought I should run so I could jump better."

"You know, I could help you jump better," said the wolf. "All I need to do is take a bite out of your leg."

He snapped at the fox and showed his teeth.

"Be careful or I will scream," the fox said. She was afraid.

But the wolf knew what would happen if the fox screamed. The dogs might come. He told the fox to leap onto the wall first. Then he followed her.

Once on top, they looked around. They saw no one. Only the well with the two buckets.

They jumped to the ground and walked over to it. The fox looked in. There was only a little water in the bottom. But there was just enough to catch the light of the moon.

"How lucky we are," said the fox. "There is a big round cheese down there. Look! Look! Did you ever see anything so beautiful?"

The wolf looked in and smiled. He thought the light from the moon was a big round cheese.

"I have never seen so much cheese before," said the wolf.

"And what do you have to say for yourself now?" asked the fox.

TALES OF ANIMALS

"I am sorry, dear friend," the wolf answered. "I am really sorry."

"Well, I am going to do one more thing," the fox said. "I want you to go down first and eat your fill."

"No! No!" exclaimed the wolf. "You should be the one who goes down in the bucket. And if you won't, I will send your head down without you."

The fox smiled. That was the answer she was waiting for.

"Well, if that's what you want," the fox said.

"Just be sure you don't eat all the cheese," the wolf said.

And the fox climbed into the bucket. She was at the bottom of the well in an instant. "Why, this is bigger and better than I thought!" she called to the wolf.

The wolf looked down into the well.

"Just bring it up quickly," he said.

"How can I? It weighs more than I do," the fox said.

"If it is so heavy, bring it up in two pieces," said the wolf.

"I have no knife," answered the fox. "You will have to come down here yourself. Then we can carry it up together."

"But how can I get down there?" asked the wolf.

"Oh, you silly thing," the fox replied. "Climb into that other bucket. There—over your head."

The wolf looked up and saw the other bucket. He pulled it down and stepped in. He weighed almost four times as much as the fox. His bucket went down very fast. At the same time, the bucket with the fox came to the top of the well.

The Fox and the Wolf

As soon as the wolf saw what had happened, he was very angry. But then he remembered the cheese.

"Now, where is that big piece of cheese?" he asked.

"The cheese?" said the fox. "Why, I am taking it home to my babies. They are too little to get food for themselves."

"You tricked me!" cried the wolf. "Just you wait! When I get out of here, I will come and find you. And I will eat you up!"

But the fox never heard him. She had already gone to the chicken house. She'd seen some fat young chickens there the day before.

"Maybe I was unkind to him," the fox said. "Oh, well. It is getting dark. And it may rain. I'd better hurry on.

"If it rains hard, the other bucket will fill with water and sink to the bottom. Then the wolf's bucket will come to the top.

"That is, if he's lucky!"

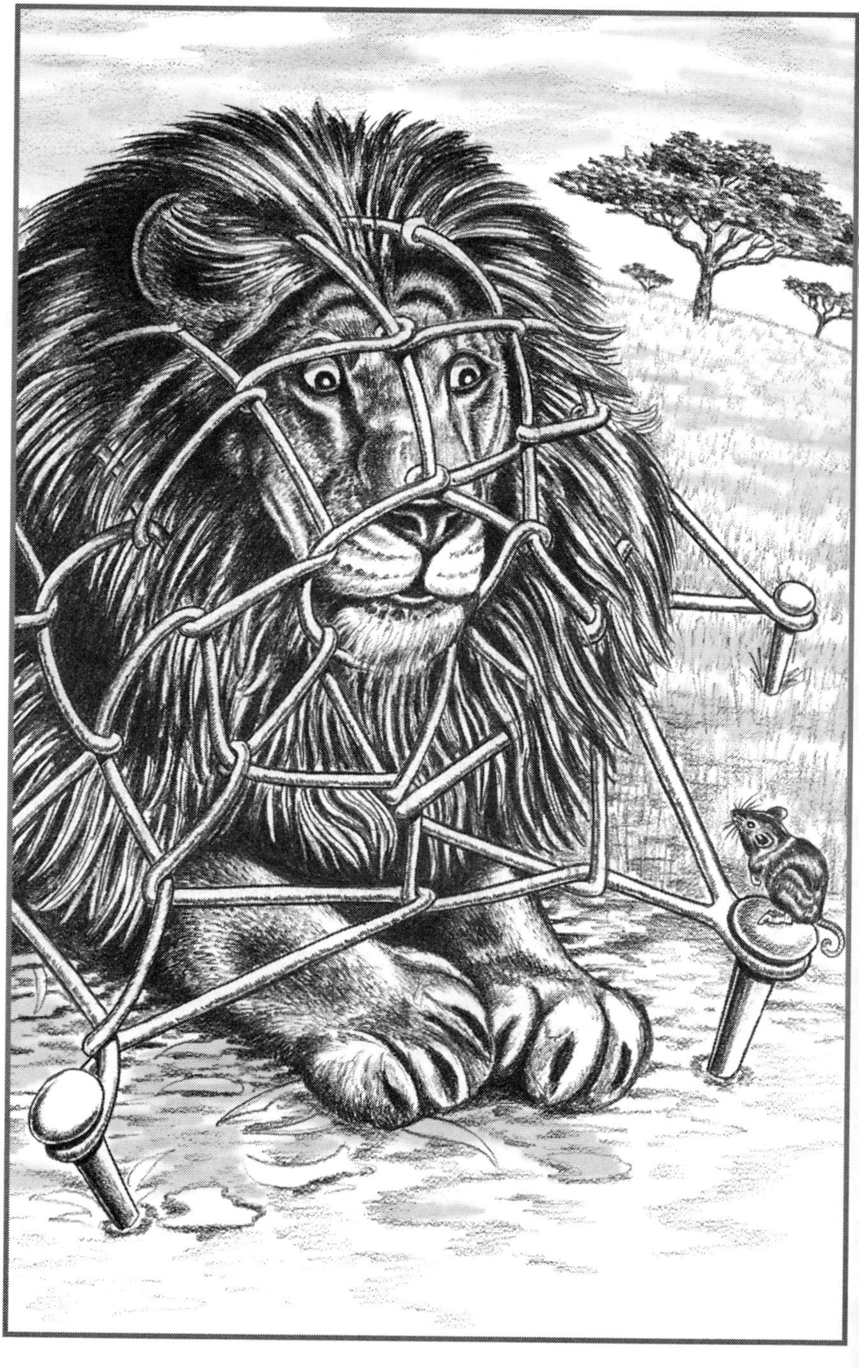

The Lion and the Mouse

A Tale from Aesop

It was a quiet night in the dark, green forest. The moon had just begun to shine through the trees.

The lion had eaten a nice, big supper. And he was fast asleep at the door of his cave. He was dreaming about all kinds of good food. Suddenly, he felt something tug at his mane.

"What's this?" he growled sleepily. He pulled up his paw. There was a tiny brown mouse!

"G-r-r-r-r!" growled the lion. "What are you doing in my mane?"

"Oh please, Mr. Lion," squeaked the mouse. "Please let me go. I didn't know you were a lion. I thought you were a haystack. I was looking for some nice hay to put in my nest."

"You silly thing!" the lion roared. "You expect me to believe that? I should eat you up."

TALES OF ANIMALS

"Please!" cried the mouse. "Forgive me. And let me go. I will pay you back someday."

The lion just laughed. "You will help me? I have never heard anything so silly. I am the king of the forest."

And with that, he dropped the tiny brown mouse into the grass. And he went back to sleep.

The next morning, the lion woke up hungry. It was a beautiful day.

"Maybe I should go hunting again in the forest," he said.

A few minutes later, he was on his way. But the lion did not know what the day would bring. Instead of being the *hunter,* he became the *hunted.*

You see, the king's hunters were looking for lions to put in the Royal Zoo. As they walked through the woods, they came upon the lion's tracks. They began to follow them. In less than an hour, they caught the lion and tied him up. Then they went to get a cage.

"Gr-r-r-r!" roared the lion. He tugged at the ropes. But he couldn't break them.

Meanwhile, the tiny mouse was running through the grass nearby.

"Gr-r-r-r!" roared the lion again. This time his roar was even louder.

"I know that voice," said the little mouse.

He began to run through the woods. Soon he came upon the lion, who was still tugging at the ropes.

The Lion and the Mouse

"Where did you come from?" the lion roared.

"Never mind. Just keep still," squeaked the mouse. "Don't move. And I will get you free, Mr. Lion."

The little mouse took the rope in his tiny teeth and began to chew. He chewed through one rope. Then another. Then another.

Suddenly, the lion pulled a paw free.

"I told you I would pay you back someday," said the mouse. "Now you see I have kept my promise."

The lion stood up. It felt so good to be free. He looked down at the little mouse.

"Will you be my friend?" the lion asked.

"Of course I will," the mouse said.

The lion picked up the mouse in his huge paw. Then he set him right on top of his soft, brown mane.

And the two friends went off into the dark, green forest.

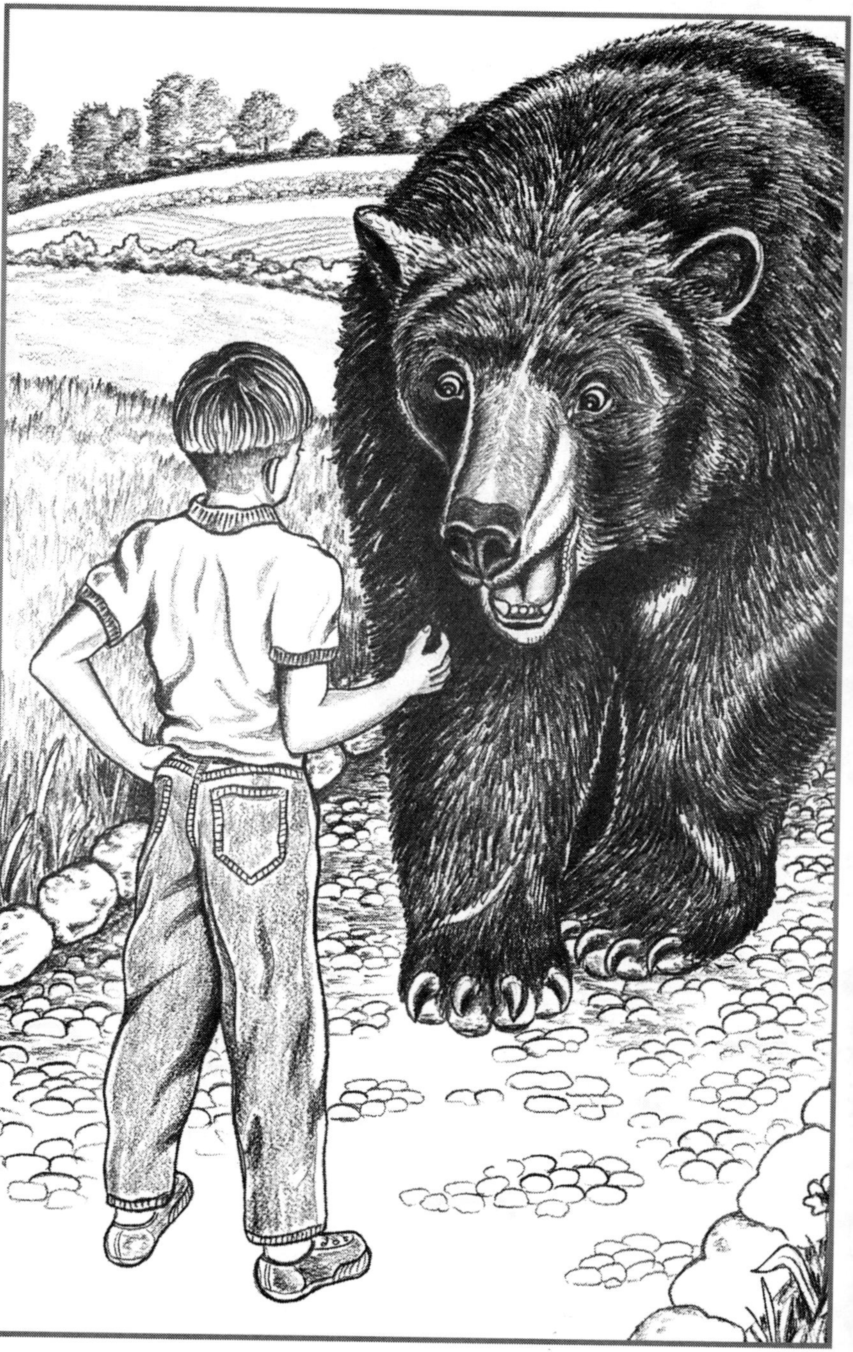

How Some Wild Animals Became Tame

Once upon a time, there was a very rich man. He wanted to invite everyone to his wedding. Even the wild animals in the forest.

So he sent invitations to the leader of the bears. And to the wolves, the foxes, the horses, and the cows. Even to the goats, the sheep, and the reindeer.

The animals were pleased. They had never been to a wedding before. So they all decided to go.

The bear was the first one to get up on the wedding day. He wanted to be on time. He brushed his teeth and combed his brown hair.

When he was ready, he left his cave. Down the road he walked. At the edge of the forest, he met a young boy.

TALES OF ANIMALS

"Where are you going, Mr. Bear?" the boy asked.

"I am going to the rich man's wedding," the bear replied.

"Oh, no!" cried the boy. "Don't go! Don't go!"

"Well, I would much rather stay at home in the forest," said the bear. "But he is so eager for me to be there."

"Please don't go, Mr. Bear," said the boy. "If you do, you will never be able to come back."

"What do you mean?" asked the bear.

"You have the most beautiful coat in the world," the boy said. "Everyone wants a bearskin. The people may kill you and take it from you."

"Hmmm," said the bear. "I had not thought of that. But then again, maybe you are just saying this. Maybe you are just mad because nobody invited you to the wedding."

"Don't be silly," said the boy. "Do as you please. It is your skin, not mine."

The boy turned away and walked down the road.

The bear watched him. He knew the boy had given him some good advice. But he was too proud to say so.

Before long, the boy got bored with walking. He turned into the woods. He thought it would be fun to jump bushes and play in the streams. Just as he got ready to jump the first bush, he met the wolf.

"Where are you going, Mr. Wolf?" asked the boy.

"To the rich man's wedding," the wolf answered.

How Some Wild Animals Became Tame

"Don't go," said the boy. "Your fur is so thick and warm. Winter will soon be here. The people may kill you and take it from you."

"What?" said the wolf. "Do you really think that might happen?"

"Yes, I do," said the boy. "But it is your business, not mine."

The boy walked away. And the wolf crawled back into his cave. He decided to think about this a little longer.

Soon the boy met the silver fox.

"You look nice today, Mr. Fox," said the boy. "Are you going to the rich man's wedding too?"

"Yes, I am," said the fox. "I have never been to a wedding before. I thought it would be fun to go."

"Listen to me," said the boy. "Stay at home. I am afraid that the rich man's dogs will hurt you."

"Really?" said the fox. "Well, I guess something like that could happen."

And the fox turned away and ran to his home.

Suddenly, the young boy heard a loud noise in the trees. A black horse came trotting by.

"Good morning, young man!" he called to the boy. "I can't stop and talk to you now. I am on my way to the rich man's wedding."

"Stop, stop, Mr. Horse!" cried the boy.

"Why? What is the matter?" asked the horse.

"If you go there, they will put ropes around your neck," said the boy. "Then you will have to work for them every day of your life."

The horse threw back his head and laughed.

"Don't be silly, young boy," he said. "I am strong. They cannot tie me up. I will always be free to run in the forest."

And the horse ran away as fast as he could. Soon he came to the rich man's house. And everything happened like the boy had said.

A man put a rope over the horse's head. And the horse fell to the ground. He struggled. But he could not get away.

The man put the horse in a cold, wet barn. The horse thought about what the boy had told him. And he was very sad.

Meanwhile, the young boy walked on. He ate some wild strawberries from a strawberry patch. And he picked some wild cherries from a tree.

Soon he came to a clearing in the forest. He saw a beautiful milk-white cow with a wreath of flowers around her neck.

"Good morning," said the cow.

"Good morning, Miss Cow," the boy answered. "Where are you going in such a hurry?"

"To the rich man's wedding," she said. "I can't talk now. I am already late. It took me a long time to make my wreath."

"Don't go!" the boy said. "Please don't go, Miss Cow! Once the people have tasted your milk, they will never let you leave."

"Don't be silly," said the cow. "What do you know? I can run twice as fast as anyone."

How Some Wild Animals Became Tame

And with that, she went on her way.

But once the cow got to the wedding, everything turned out just as the boy had said.

The wedding guests had heard of cow's milk. And they asked her to give them some. Before long, they took her to the barn.

Later they tied a long rope around her head. And they let her walk in the grass. But they would not let her go back to the forest.

The same thing happened to the goat. And the sheep.

Finally, the boy met the reindeer.

"Where are you going, Mr. Reindeer?" the boy asked.

"I am going to the rich man's wedding," the reindeer said. "He wants me to be there."

"Don't go! Please don't go!" the boy said. "When you get there, they will keep you. Because no animal or bird is as strong as you."

"That is why I am safe," the reindeer said. And he, too, was on his way.

But the reindeer never came back. Neither did any of the other animals. They all thought they knew more than the young boy.

If they had listened to him, the animals and their children would still be free today.

How Some Wild Animals Became Tame

The Play

48

The Play: How Some Wild Animals Became Tame

Cast of Characters

Narrator
Young Boy
The Bear
The Wolf
The Fox
The Horse
Farmhand
The Cow
The Reindeer

Setting: The forest

Act One

Narrator: Once upon a time, there was a very rich man. He was planning to marry. He was so happy. And he wanted everyone to come to the wedding. Even the wild animals who lived in the forest.

So one day, he sat down and wrote invitations. He wrote to the leader of the bears. He wrote to the wolves, the foxes, and the horses. And he wrote to the cows, the goats, the sheep, and the reindeer.

The animals were surprised to be invited. They had never been to a wedding before. They thought it would be fun. So each one wrote back to say he would be there.

The wedding day came. The bear got up very early. He wanted to be on time. Besides, he had a long way to go. But at the edge of the forest, he met a young boy.

TALES OF ANIMALS

Young Boy: Good morning, Mr. Bear. Where are you going on this fine day?

The Bear: To the rich man's wedding.

Young Boy: To a wedding?

The Bear: Yes, a wedding. Of course, I would much rather be at home. But the rich man wanted me to be there. So I couldn't say no.

Young Boy: Oh, Mr. Bear! Please don't go! You have the most beautiful fur in the world. It's just the kind everyone wants. The people may kill you and take it from you.

The Bear: Well, maybe you are just saying this because nobody invited you.

Young Boy: What? Why, that's silly, Mr. Bear. But do as you please. It's your coat, not mine.

Narrator: The boy turned and walked away. The bear thought about what the boy had said. He knew the boy was right. But he was too proud to say so. In any case, he walked back to his cave and stayed there.

Act Two

Narrator: The boy walked into the woods. Here he could jump over bushes and play in the streams. But just as he came to the first bush, he met the wolf.

Young Boy: Where are you going, Mr. Wolf?

The Wolf: Oh, just to the rich man's wedding. Of course, I'd rather stay home. But I thought I should go.

The Play: How Some Wild Animals Became Tame

Young Boy: Don't go, Mr. Wolf! Please listen to me. Your coat is so thick and warm. Winter is not far away. They will kill you and take it from you for sure.

The Wolf: What? Do you *really* think they would do that to me?

Young Boy: Yes. Yes, I do. But it is your business, not mine.

Narrator: The boy turned and walked away. The wolf stood there for a few minutes. Then he went back to his cave to think about it.

Soon, the boy met the fox.

Young Boy: Well, good morning, Mr. Fox. You look very nice today. Are you going to the rich man's wedding too?

The Fox: Yes. Yes, I am. It is a long way to go. But I thought it would be nice of me. I hear everyone in the forest is going.

Young Boy: Well, Mr. Fox, I hope you will take my advice and stay at home. I'm afraid that the rich man's dogs will tear you to pieces.

The Fox: Hmmm. I know such things have happened before. So I guess I should think this over.

Narrator: As the fox walked away, the young boy heard a loud noise behind an oak tree. A black horse trotted by.

The Horse: Neigh, hey, hey! Good morning, boy! I can't talk to you now. I'm in a hurry. I have to go to the rich man's wedding. They are waiting for me.
Young Boy: Stop, Mr. Horse!
The Horse: What is the matter?
Young Boy: Please don't go. I know you are big and strong, Mr. Horse. But the people will catch you. And they'll put a rope around your neck. Then they will make you work for them the rest of your life.
The Horse: Neigh, hey! You make me laugh! As you said, I am big and strong. All the ropes in the world cannot hold me. I will always be free.

Narrator: And with that, the horse shook his long tail and ran away. The young boy was very sad. Nobody wanted to believe him.

Act Three

Narrator: It was a beautiful day for a wedding. The sun was shining. Some of the guests were there when the horse ran up. As the horse looked around, he knew he was bigger and stronger than any of them. But just then, someone threw a rope over his head.

The Horse: Neigh, hey! What are you doing? I am a guest at this wedding. And where are you taking me?
Farmhand: Be quiet, Mr. Horse. I'm taking you to the barn. We have lots of work for you to do on this farm.

The Play: How Some Wild Animals Became Tame

The Horse: Oh please, no! Please don't take me to that cold, dark place. Please take the rope from my neck. Let me go back to the forest!

Farmhand: You heard me, Mr. Horse. Be quiet. If you are good today, I will give you a carrot. Or maybe a lump of sugar.

Narrator: The horse lay down and began to cry. He wished he had listened to the wise words of the young boy. What would ever become of him?

Meanwhile, the young boy had walked on. He picked some wild cherries from a tree. He ate some strawberries from a bush. Soon he came upon a beautiful milk-white cow.

The Cow: Why, good morning, young man. How are you today?

Young Boy: Good morning, Miss Cow. I am fine, thank you. You look so nice with that beautiful wreath of flowers around your neck. Where are you going?

The Cow: To the rich man's wedding. And I'm late. It took me so long to make this wreath. I'm sorry I don't have time to talk with you.

Young Boy: To the wedding? Oh, Miss Cow! Please don't go. Once the people have tasted your milk, they will never let you leave.

The Cow: Oh, don't be silly. They would never be able to keep me. Why, I can run two times as fast as anyone else.

TALES OF ANIMALS

Narrator: Miss Cow walked away. And the boy walked on. But once the cow got to the rich man's house, everything happened as the boy had said it would. The people held the cow's horns so she could not use them. Then they put her in the barn with the horse. And the same thing happened to the goat and the sheep. The young boy had tried to warn them too. Then came the reindeer.

Young Boy: Where are you going, Mr. Reindeer?
The Reindeer: I have been invited to the rich man's wedding.
Young Boy: Oh, no. Not you too! Please don't go, Mr. Reindeer. When you get there, the people will keep you there. No other animal or bird is as strong as you.
The Reindeer: Silly boy! That's just why I am going. I will be quite safe. I am so strong that no one can tie me up. And I am so fast that not even an arrow can catch me.

Narrator: With that, the young boy walked out of the forest. He felt very sad.

Meanwhile, the reindeer ran off to the rich man's house. When he got there, he was put in the barn. Sadly, all the animals had thought they knew more than the little boy. Now they were very lonely. But they had lots of time to think. Had they listened to their young friend, they would be happy. And the animals and their children would not be working on the farm—or in a cage at the zoo—today.